The Battle of Hastings 1066 and the story of Battle Abbey

Plantagenet Somerset Fry

Battle Abbey lies on the historic site of the Battle of Hastings. It was here that the crucial engagement between the English army under King Harold and the invading troops of William, Duke of Normandy, took place on 14 October 1066 – the most celebrated date in English History.

Some fifteen years earlier Edward the Confessor had promised the English crown to Duke William, but on Edward's death, the pledge was broken and Harold was proclaimed king.

William, by invading England, sought to assert his right to the crown. At the Battle of Hastings, King Harold fell mortally wounded and the Normans triumphed.

In penance for the slaughter, William I (as Duke William became) built an abbey on the site of the battle and he directed that the church high altar should occupy the very spot where King Harold fell.

This guide opens with a tour of the battlefield and an account of the Battle of Hastings. The visitor is then guided round the surviving ruins of the abbey.

CONTENTS

FRONT Scene (top) from the Bayeux Tapestry depicting the Battle, with (below) the abbey gatehouse.

Published by English Heritage

Edited by Ken Osborne, designed by Martin Atcherley of Design Guide, and typeset by Keldia Printing Co. Ltd. in ITC Century Book.

Copyright © English Heritage 1990 Reprinted 1994,1997
Printed in England by Keldia Printing Co. Ltd
C45, 12/97
ISBN 1 15074 185 9

The Battle of Hastings 1066: a tour of the battlefield

PREVIOUS PAGE English foot soldiers defending a small hillock against the merciless onslaught of the Norman cavalry

BELOW Preceded by volleys of arrows from the Norman archers, Duke William's mounted knights (left) charge into the English line. Harold's housecarls (right) form shield-walls. At their side a solitary English archer raises his bow.

The Battle of Hastings was described by several chroniclers of the time and soon afterwards, and various key episodes were picked out by the weavers of the Bayeux Tapestry. But medieval chroniclers were not given to blow-by-blow accounts of warfare (unlike present-day war correspondents). So the actual sequence of events has to a great extent to be guesswork.

The Norman strength was probably about 7000 men, including 2000–3000 cavalry. The English army is thought to have been much the same size. But there was one critical difference. Norman cavalry fought from horseback, wielding sword and thrusting lance. Those of the English who rode to battle dismounted and fought on foot.

With hindsight we can see an immediate advantage for William. No doubt he appreciated it, too, but he was not so over-confident to think that the battle would be a walk-over. The reputation of the English infantry stood high.

The English occupied the crest of the ridge on Battle Hill facing southwards and stretching east to west some 600–800 yards, from the junction of the Hastings and Sedlescombe roads to the present car park.

YOUR TOUR OF THE BATTLEFIELD *begins at the first table model which stands a few yards from the visitor centre. This is at the western end of the English line. The walk around the battlefield is quite long. Elderly visitors may prefer to view the battlefield from the terrace (Table Model 2).*

The English line consisted of 10 to 12 close-packed ranks of infantry and archers. Somewhere in the middle, the English

commander, King Harold II, stood surrounded by his housecarls, an elite bodyguard of crack troops who carried the dreaded two-handed battle-axe and who were among the best troops in Europe.

Duke William positioned the opposing forces near the bottom of the south slope of the ridge and reaching upwards again on the slope on his side. His front was about 400 yards from the English front-most rank and he ranged three lines, first archers, and perhaps a few crossbowmen with them, then heavy infantry (many wearing coats of mail) and behind these the cavalry. The lines were divided into three blocks (or lateral divisions): on the west the Breton volunteers, in the centre the Normans, with the duke himself, and on the east almost at right angles and on an incline, the French (Aquitainians and others).

CONTINUE YOUR TOUR *by following the path southwards, then turning east through a gate in some pretty woodland, to a second gate and out in the western edge of the battlefield. Here you find the third table model, in front of the trees. This is the area where the right wing of* *the English forces engaged the Breton infantry troops of William's army, during the first attack launched by the duke.*

Walk straight down the slope with the fence on your right until you come to rough ground rising to a knoll, covered with gorse and threaded by a winding path which skirts south of a marsh-encircled small pond in front of the knoll. On the knoll is the fourth table model.

The Bretons probably occupied the knoll soon after the first attack launched by William at about nine in the morning. He sent his infantry divisions uphill against the English line, the Bretons struggling up and over the knoll only to find themselves pressed very hard by an English force which had the advantage of a downhill run against them. These first assaults made little impact, and William signalled the knights forward, lances couched, hard-riding up the slope in the direction of the strong English line.

The knights fared little better, and in several sectors they had to turn back to regroup, a manoeuvre difficult to carry out in a hurry without creating an impression of disordered retreat.

A housecarl wields his battle axe, his sword remaining in his scabbard. Alongside him, a peasant soldier carries only a spear.

RIGHT During the course of the battle, a rumour spread through the Norman ranks that Duke William had been wounded. Here William is shown raising his helmet to his men to prove that he is unharmed. In front of him rides a knight carrying the Papal Banner.

BELOW During the final stages of the battle, the English line was broken by a counter-attack. Volleys of Norman arrows were followed by cavalry charges and close hand-to-hand fighting. The tapestry depicts Harold struck in the eye by an arrow. Wounded, he is cut down with a sword. 'Harold the King is killed' reads the Latin inscription. The English army, demoralised and weakened, flees, leaving only the housecarls to fight a rearguard action in the approaching twilight.

TURN RIGHT *down on the south side of the knoll, a steepish drop until you reach a straight flight of wood-edged earth steps descending to the lower part of the field. Continue towards the north edge of a small lake (a later feature on the other side of the fence and not part of the battlefield). Swing left towards a wooden bridge across a stream leading from the lake into marshland. Go south of the marshland. to another gate and another bridge across the marsh. Here is the fifth table model.*

In this marshy area the Bretons, thrown by the force of the English assault on them, set up the cry that William himself had been killed, which caused further disarray in the western sector and even affected the Norman centre.

Duke William was seriously alarmed. He rode about the ranks raising his helmet to show the army that he was by no means dead. While that was going on, the English broke their ranks and charged downhill in pursuit, but, sword in hand, William led a vigorous counter-attack and many English were cut down. The crisis was not yet over, however, and William followed with a major assault – again uphill and again with cavalry – crashing into the solid wall of the English defence. The resistance seemed as strong as ever.

GO ON FROM TABLE MODEL 5 *to Table Model 6. On your right the ground rises.*

This is where the Norman army had assembled before the battle. Possibly it is where William first rallied his men and began his counter-attack, as one chronicler wrote: 'one side attacking with all mobility, the other withstanding as though rooted to the soil.'

Then came the moment when William tried the feigned flight manoeuvre, one with which he had become familiar earlier in his career. This was for small units of mounted knights, *conrois*, to pretend to pull out, gallop

off and entice the enemy to break ranks in pursuit, then wheel round and cut down the pursuers. It was a manoeuvre that with practice was well within the capacity of eleventh-century knights who were accustomed to spending much of their time training and exercising. Undoubtedly it worked at the battle near Hastings. Indeed, one chronicler of the early twelfth century, William of Malmesbury, reckoned it proved the turning point of the battle.

Yet still the main English line held, straddling the lower parts of the slope below the abbey.

CONTINUE YOUR TOUR *from Table Model 6 past Table Model 7, following the path. This was the ground held so resolutely by the English and only yielded yard by yard in the evening as the light began to fade. Climb upwards towards the abbey, following, as it were, the footsteps of the gradually yielding English as one by one they fell.*

The last phase of the battle took place further up the ridge where the ruins of the abbey church can now be seen. The final push launched by William was preceded by devastating volleys of arrows by wave after wave of archers shooting high into the sky because they were firing uphill. It was the shooting that brought the collapse of the English army that evening. One arrow struck King Harold in or near the eye, wounding though not killing him, as is so graphically shown on the Bayeux Tapestry. His brothers had already been killed, and many of his housecarls with them. As the injured king

tried desperately to pull the arrow out of his head, some Norman knights came upon him and cut him down with their swords.

Swiftly the news of his end spread through the now straggling and much thinned ranks of the English. They broke up and fled, many of them chased by the Normans, among them William himself on horseback (on his fourth horse of that day, for three had been killed under him).

YOUR TOUR OF THE BATTLEFIELD *ends just below the southernmost buildings of the abbey, on the Lower Terrace in front of the undercroft (basement rooms) of the guest range, by Table Model 2 in front of one of the undercroft chambers. In the chamber is a model of the whole battlefield showing both armies facing each other as they might have been at 9 am on that October day in 1066. Look southwards from the Lower Terrace and view the whole battlefield, much as it might have appeared to Harold and his army before action began. The Lower Terrace is where you join the tour of the abbey ruins (see page 8).*

(see page 8).

A shower of arrows, fired high into the air, preceded each Norman attack. The professional Norman archers used short or Danish bows and came within a hundred yards of the English line before releasing their hail of arrows.

Scenes from the eleventh-century Bayeux Tapestry in this book are reproduced by courtesy of the Michael Holford Library

Battle of Hastings, 14 October 1066

In this reconstruction illustration by Jason Askew, the battle is shown at its fiercest and the horror of the slaughter is apparent. Waves of Norman cavalry (left) attempt to penetrate the resolute English line (right), the horsemen's approach tempered by the danger to their mounts in hand-to-hand fighting. Significant improvements in saddles, spurs and stirrups enabled the Norman knights to ride into battle, whereas the English knights generally dismounted to fight on foot. Shields were of two designs, round for infantrymen and elongated for mounted soldiers. In addition to leather thongs that fastened the shield to the arm, horsemen had a strap around the shoulder. Personal insignia were emblazoned on shields, including representations of mythical beasts. Knights wore heavy chain mail, but many of the peasant soldiers went into battle wearing simple tunics. In the fury of conflict, a sword could split a man's skull and the two handed axe could sever a man's head.

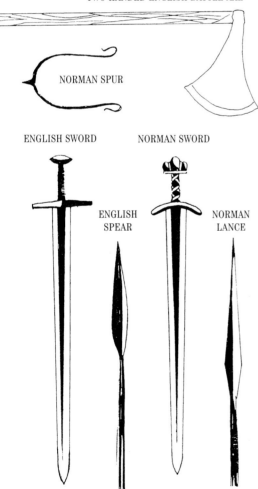

TWO-HANDED ENGLISH BATTLE AXE

NORMAN SPUR

ENGLISH SWORD

NORMAN SWORD

ENGLISH SPEAR

NORMAN LANCE

ENGLISH HERITAGE

Battle Abbey, 1070–1538: a tour of the Abbey Ruins

Lower Terrace

Your tour of the abbey ruins begins at the west end of the **Lower Terrace,** the southernmost part of the abbey. Walking eastwards along it you can share the view over the battlefield on the right that Harold himself might have seen before the action and William the morning afterwards. On the left, there was then nothing in the way of buildings, only rising scrubland ground, but within five years William had ordered the building of an abbey on the site, to atone for the death of so many people at his great victory of 1066. By about 1100, much of the original abbey was finished, including the church and the chapter house. But in the thirteenth century there were to be major alterations and enlargements, and with this in mind you can continue along the Lower Terrace.

On your left is the high wall of a **medieval barn.** This is where the cellarer, the abbey storekeeper, stored corn and other produce from the abbey farms. Next to the barn is the thirteenth-century **undercroft** range (an undercroft is a vaulted chamber used for storage, accommodation or as an office) forming part of the basement of the abbey's **guest range** where friends of the abbot and other visitors stayed.

After the monastery was dissolved in 1538–39, the guest block upstairs was rebuilt by Sir Anthony Browne, to whom Henry VIII gave the abbey. The new range was reputedly to accommodate Princess Elizabeth and Prince Edward, the king's children, but in fact neither ever stayed there. Two corner towers were added to the guest block's west end. Only the towers and the steps from the Terrace to the block remain.

Continue eastwards along the terrace to the end of the undercroft range and veer left where you see a flight of steps, sandwiched between the east wall of a small garden and the south-west corner of the dorter (dormitory), which is the southern part of the east range. The **kitchen garden** is open only in the school holidays (via an opening in the east wall). It contains the remains of the tiled floor of a conservatory.

The **dorter** block is a mid-thirteenth-century rebuilding and enlargement of the original dormitory of the early twelfth century. It is unusually tall at its southern end

ABOVE South front of the undercroft beneath the guest range

ENGLISH HERITAGE

BELOW Bird's eye view by Terry Ball of the abbey and school buildings. Compare the illustration on pages 12-13.

Car park and visitor centre

Battlefield

Wall of medieval barn

Lower Terrace

Undercroft of Guest Range

BELOW South end of the dorter range

ENGLISH HERITAGE

Great Gatehouse

Courthouse

Transepts and crossing of church

Chapter House

N
W E
S

Battle Abbey School (PRIVATE)

Site of first Altar at the spot where Harold fell

Abbot's Great Hall (PART OF SCHOOL)

Parlour

Chevet (apse) with crypt chapels

Cloister

Battlemented precinct wall

ENGLISH HERITAGE

Kitchen garden (OPEN ONLY IN SCHOOL HOLIDAYS)

Slype

Site of Infirmary

Kitchen (Block)

Novices' Room

Reredorter

A DETAILED PLAN OF THE ABBEY CHURCH AND ORIGINAL BUILDINGS APPEARS ON PAGE 24

Frater (Dining-hall)

Dorter (Dormitory)

Monks' Common Room

because the building was erected on a sloping site and had to accommodate two storeys, each tall enough all the way along to provide headroom. This was the result of the Conqueror's determination that the abbey church itself should occupy the spot where King Harold fell.

Adjoining the south end of the dorter block, at right angles to it, is the abbey's **reredorter,** or latrine block. Note the line of high, rounded arches acting as the south wall, and just north of the line see the reredorter's main drain. The arches once supported a row of latrine seats which were along the first floor of the reredorter. Notice also the interesting doorways where the reredorter joins the dorter block, providing direct access to the latrines. Monks usually carried out their morning and evening ablutions together *en masse,* as they had a tightly packed timetable each day.

East Range

Return to the steps between the walled garden and the dorter block, and go up to the doorway into the lower storey of the dorter block, on right. This takes you into what was probably the **novices' room,** where people new to the monastic life and anxious to train to be accepted as monks at the abbey gathered for the teaching and leisure periods of their novitiate every day. During their year's training, novices were kept separate from the rest of the abbey community, except in the church and frater (dining hall).

At Battle Abbey the novices' room has a particularly high vaulted ceiling which is supported by a central row of graceful pillars, so that the dormitory floor above could be level. Among interesting features to see are the sharply sloping window openings which let more light in, and the substantial fireplace in the south wall with its back made of layers of mortared roof tiles, above which are the marks of its large hood. The smoke from the fire rose into a shaft inside the buttress behind the south wall outside.

In the south-east corner a narrow doorway leading to an equally narrow curving flight of steps leads to a latrine.

Leave the novices' room via the flight of steps in the north-east corner, noting on the right a delightful arched recess (niche) that may have stored books for novices. Through the doorway you come into a narrow east-west aligned room, also with vaulted ceiling. This may have been the abbey library, though it was not usual for monasteries to have all their books in one room until later in the Middle Ages.

The doorway on the shorter east wall led to the **infirmary** buildings (where sick and elderly monks were housed and received treatment) on the east side of the dorter, of which there are practically no remains. North of the library (?) is the **slype,** a narrow barrel-vaulted passage running through the dorter block at lower storey level from the west where it led from the kitchen block (see page 11) to the infirmary buildings. Note especially the fine rounded-arch doorways at each end, which still have some of the ironwork of the door hinges in the masonry.

Cross the slype to yet another vaulted chamber, this time one with two rows of marble pillars supporting a fine rib-vaulted ceiling. Here, the ceiling is much lower than that in the novices' room. This was the **monks' common room** where they enjoyed recreations. In cold weather, warmth must have been provided by portable braziers brought in at allotted leisure periods.

As you enter the common room, notice the fine carved heads on some of the corbels along the walls, which support the arches of the vaulted ceiling.

The common room is lit by five lancet windows (tall, narrow pointed) along the east wall, but curiously there are rounded top windows. Go out of the common room through the more northerly rounded arch door on the west side, up steps into the south-east corner of the **cloister.** The cloister was a covered walk or arcade that ran around the sides of an open quadrangle, which linked the central abbey buildings with the abbey church (see page 12).

West Range

Looking out westwards across the **cloister garth** (or courtyard) you can see along the east wall of the **west range** traces of thirteenth and fifteenth-century vaulting that remain from the claustral (cloister) walk. This walk was once covered by a tiled sloping roof supported on polished marble pillars interspersed with arcading and was paved with large slabs of stone.

The west range contained the **abbot's great hall** of the thirteenth century, which had its own undercroft where the cellarer stored food and other supplies. The abbot's great chamber was further west at right angles to the south end of the hall. These quarters were rebuilt and altered in later centuries and they now constitute part of the

ABOVE *Reredorter or latrine block. The upper doorways in the back wall give direct access from the monks' dorter or dormitory on the first floor.*

BELOW *The novices' room with its fine vaulted ceiling.*

ENGLISH HERITAGE

A. F. KERSTING

ENGLISH HERITAGE

ABOVE *East front of the abbot's great hall (now part of the school) viewed from the cloister. Note the remains of the beautiful claustral vaulting along the wall.*

present Battle Abbey School and are not normally open to visitors.

The south side of the cloister is in the school grounds, but note the foundations of the **frater** (monks' dining hall), which has its plan marked out in the grass. This building was one of the major alterations of the thirteenth century. So was the monastic **kitchen block** immediately to the south of the frater, the plan of which is also marked out in the grass. The kitchen was a large, square building, two storeys tall, with a central cooking area enclosed by hearths, with ranges on each of the four sides. The kitchen survived the demolitions of the period of the Dissolution of the Monasteries and immediately afterwards. In fact it was not pulled down until the 1680s.

Return north-eastwards to the chapter house in the east range of the cloister. The chapter house originally abutted on to the south wall of the south transept of the first abbey church.

Just beyond the north end of the long dorter block there is a space with some foundations. This was the **parlour**, an original building reconstructed in the thirteenth century. The parlour was a room-cum-passage (it had an eastern door to the infirmary buildings and western doors direct into the cloister). Here, monks could talk among themselves, though usually on important matters only. Silence was meant to be observed elsewhere on the abbey buildings.

Standing on this open space and looking south you can see the first floor of the dorter block, the dormitory. This very large room, now roofless, was intended to accommodate up to 140 monks, but seldom housed more than half that number. The dorter was roofed with wooden shingles from the first days but in the fourteenth century the shingles were replaced with roof tiles.

In its first years it may have been unheated. Fireplaces were later on inserted in the walls (you can see some of them) and the room was divided into partitioned cubicles. To get to the dorter from the cloister you went up a flight of steps to a door along the west wall close to the north-west corner (the doorway is visible to-day). Long after the abbey itself was largely demolished following the Dissolution of the Monasteries in 1538, the dorter which survived well into the nineteenth century was converted into a block of stables which were reached by means of an earthen ramp to the first floor at the north end.

Chapter House

Turn north again and walk over to the footings that adjoin the parlour, noticeable from the rounded east end and from traces of projecting buttresses round the outside of this next building. This was the **Chapter House**, the administrative centre of the abbey. Here, the monks met once a day to discuss the abbey's business affairs and to listen to the reading from the rule of St Benedict, founder of Western monasticism in the sixth century AD. The first chapter house had been finished by about 1100: in the thirteenth century it was altered to incorporate new windows (possibly of Early English pointed style). Today you can see some of the stone benches that encircled the north and south sides of the apsidal east end.

Abbey Church

The first abbey church, of which very little remains, was completed in 1094 and consecrated by the archbishop of Canterbury in the presence of the Conqueror's son, William II (Rufus). The present wall along the north side of the cloister is partly the original walling of this first church. The first church was 225ft long. It had a central **crossing** with north and south **transepts.** The **nave** (west end) had seven bays. The church was probably the first major Norman church to be completed in England.

At its east end, the church originally had a rounded **apse** (semi-circular end) which contained three radiating chapels and, inside, an **ambulatory** (semi-circular walkway flanked by pillars). Slightly west of the apse end was the **high altar**, positioned more or less exactly where King Harold fell. You can see today a square stone in the grass at the spot, commemorating Harold's death. The position of the apse and other parts of the plan of the church are marked in the grass.

In the later thirteenth century, after the cloister and its linked buildings were

ABOVE An illustration by Ivan Lapper showing the abbey as it might have appeared in the early sixteenth century. The community was self-sufficient in produce from its surrounding lands. It was also the biggest employer in the neighbourhood The west courtyard would have been an area of bustling daily activity, as is suggested here. The abbey was also accustomed to entertaining guests regularly judging by the size of the guest range.

KEY TO ILLUSTRATION
1 Great gatehouse
2 Abbot's house
3 Medieval Barn
4 Guest range
5 Dorter range
6 Reredorter
7 Chapter house
8 Cloister
9 Frater
10 Kitchens
11 Church: high altar on site where Harold was killed.
12 Church: east end remodelled in thirteenth century
13 North precinct wall
14 Courthouse (built mid-sixteenth century)

ENGLISH HERITAGE

The Monks' daily timetable at Battle Abbey

The daily life of the monks at Battle Abbey was ordered by a strict timetable, or *horarium*, based on the rule of St Benedict, founder of Western monasticism. It was built around prayer, study and work, and it varied according to the seasons and whether it was a fasting or an ordinary day.

The day began at about 2am with a summons by a church bell to the first service, Nocturns, followed at dawn by Matins, and then a third service, Lauds, with short intervals for prayer between each. The monks then left the church for the cloister area for study and reading. At about 8 am they went up the stairs in the east range to the dorter, along to the reredorter to wash, and back to the dorter to change into day clothes.

When they were ready, they went down to the frater for a light breakfast of bread and ale, and after that, to the church again for the first Mass of the day. When that was over, they gathered in the chapter house for a reading of a chapter of the Rule of St Benedict (hence the name of the building) and a discussion of the temporal affairs of the community. Here sins would be confessed and punishments decreed. Two hours of study and reading followed, and then they returned to church for High Mass.

By about 2pm most monks would have been extremely hungry – though they would not have said so aloud! – and at that hour they sat down in the frater for the day's main meal, in which they would have meat on three days a week, and fish or eggs on the other four. Each day they also had bread, fruit, vegetables grown by the community in fields nearby, and perhaps ale again.

After the meal they would rest or read, then work, perhaps in the fields, or gardens, or in the library, or cellars, or work shops, depending on their skills or the needs of the day. At sunset a bell would summon them to Vespers (evening service), followed by a final snack in the frater. The day's last service was Compline, in the church, and after that all the monks went to bed – until the 2am summons by bell to the church for the next day's first service.

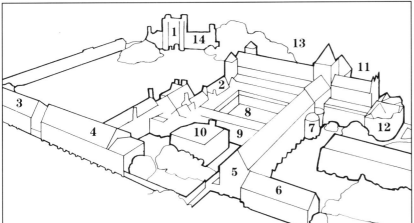

reconstructed, the abbey church itself was enlarged. The western part (nave and transepts) was probably left largely alone, but the whole of the original east end pulled down and a new, longer east end built in its place. This included a seven-bay **choir** (eastern arm of church), at the end of which was a *chevet* (from the French *chevet*, an apse) containing five radiating chapels. Because the site sloped away eastwards, it was possible to give the chapels a **crypt chapel** underneath each. You can go down one or other of two narrow flights of steps into the crypt area and see the lay-out.

Leave the crypt and head for the north **precinct wall** around the abbey buildings, flanked in front by shrubs and trees. This wall continues westwards some distance. You will see its wall-walk and protecting battlements, fortifications that were added in the fourteenth century, when the Great Gatehouse was rebuilt partly as a defence against French raids (see page 23). In front of the wall for some of the way is the Camellia Walk, a short avenue of camellia trees. The precinct wall led to the Courthouse, a sixteenth century re-building of what were previously quarters for the abbey almoner, an official who was in charge of helping the poor and the sick of the neighbourhood outside the abbey. Much of his help was in distributing small sums of money (alms). He also handed out old clothes and footwear discarded by the monks to poor people and orphans.

Great Gatehouse

The **Courthouse** abuts on to the Great Gatehouse which is the last building of the abbey you see as you return to the car park. In some senses it is the star attraction of the whole abbey ruins. At present it is not open to the public whilst archaeological work is in progress.

The **Great Gatehouse** was built in about 1338–39. It was erected beside the original much smaller and simpler Norman entrance gate of the late eleventh century, and it incorporated parts of the earlier building. The Great Gatehouse was built during the opening years of the Hundred Years War between England and France (1337–1453), when the counties of Sussex and Kent were constantly being raided by French privateers. It was the abbey's contribution to local defence (see page 23) and it was powerfully defensive, especially when considered in conjunction with the strengthened precinct wall with which it is linked (this wall probably enclosed

ENGLISH HERITAGE

ABOVE Two finely carved bosses in the fourteenth-century great gatehouse, which are said to represent the faces of Duke William and King Harold.

OPPOSITE The great gatehouse. Its battlemented turrets and walls are a reminder that it was built at the start of the Hundred Years War (1337–1453) when the abbey needed to be defended against French raiders.

most if not all of the abbey in the fourteenth century).

The Great Gatehouse is regarded as one of the finest medieval monastic gatehouses in England, and it looks particularly formidable as it comes into view on your way up to the High Street to visit the abbey. It is a rectangular building with octagonal corner turrets. The two southern turrets have staircases up to the two upper storeys over the gatehouse's two entrances which are two vaulted passages side by side. The eastern passage is wider and taller than the western one which was intended for pedestrians only. The gatehouse was fortified with battlements along all four sides. It was equipped with cross-slot arrow loops with round end-holes; you can see eight of these in the two southern towers alone. And the gatehouse was built with walls 3 ft to 4 ft thick in places.

This military looking building is, however, distinctive for its outside decoration, some of it original, some of it renovation. Particularly interesting are the band of decorative arcading (rows of arches close side by side) on both north and south faces, and spreading round the four corner turrets, and the second-storey two-light windows above, also on each face.

The vaulted gate-passages should be seen for their fine decorated arch bosses (projecting ornament placed where vault ribs meet, to disguise the join). These include two human heads facing northwards. The northerly head is of a glum-looking man said locally to be King Harold looking anxiously northwards for reinforcements that never came, and the other is said to be a smiling Duke William who knows he has won the battle – and the throne!

The first storey of the gatehouse is reached by the staircase in the south-east turret and this has its own portcullis, which underlines the high defensiveness of the building. This storey consists of a large well-lit room, once the principal chamber in a suite of rooms. These rooms now house an exhibition about the history of the abbey.

The simpler building on the west is of the same fourteenth-century building period and it incorporates what remains of the original Norman entrance. The building was probably accommodation for the gatehouse keeper, and it also contains latrines.

Your tour ends at the south-west side of the Great Gatehouse, which is near the car park.

Why the Normans invaded England

ABOVE *King Edward the Confessor, with his family and friends. From a later manuscript.*

BRITISH LIBRARY

The death of Edward the Confessor

On Thursday 5 January 1066, Edward the Confessor, King of England since 1042, died at Westminster, perhaps within a stone's throw of the abbey church of St Peter, which he had built and consecrated there.

Hardly a day later he was buried in the abbey, and within hours Harold Godwineson, earl of Wessex, Edward's brother-in-law and the most powerful man in the kingdom, was crowned there as King Harold II. The dying Edward may have bequeathed him his kingdom, yet one source says that Edward 'commended' his queen (Harold's sister) and kingdom to Harold's 'protection', whilst another states that Harold was 'elected thereto'.

Harold was not of royal blood but he did command the royal army and seems to have had no difficulty in getting the support of a sizeable number of English magnates, though some in the north did not accept him. These he sought to win over by a quick visit to Northumbria, taking with him Wulfstan, bishop of Worcester. Harold even went so far as to marry Edith, sister of Morcar, earl of Northumbria.

His position seemed as good as it could be. But the Anglo-Saxon Chronicle says that he was not to endure a tranquil reign. Why?

BELOW *The Bayeux Tapestry records the death of Edward the Confessor and the coronation of Harold, Earl of Wessex, as King of England.*

Duke William of Normandy's claim to the throne

On the other side of the English Channel, in northern France, William, duke of Normandy, distant kinsman of the Confessor (his great-great-aunt was Edward's mother), had been spending his New Year of 1066 worrying about Edward's health, for it was known that the English King was dying. William was also thinking what he would do with the kingdom he fully expected to inherit, for not only was he a blood-heir of the Confessor, he had also been promised the succession by Edward 15 years earlier, in 1051, a promise confirmed that year by Robert, then archbishop of Canterbury, and reinforced in 1064 by Harold Godwineson himself.

When he heard of Edward's death and of what is regarded by pro-Norman historians as Harold's *coup d'état*, William was taken by surprise. He was also affronted. Though he protested to the English court, he knew he would be ignored, and it is certain that his immediate reaction was to consider asserting his claim by force.

This would entail a seaborne invasion, but he had Viking blood in his veins and was not daunted by that. Yet he grasped that it would be a very substantial operation and that it had to succeed. Preparations must be made very soundly. Special ships would have to be built. Thousands of horses, strong enough to stand a long and possibly stormy sea-journey, would have to be found, stabled near the harbour and kept in fit condition.

The logistics of preparing the invasion were not the only problem. William had to secure the support of his vassal lords and

knights in Normandy, and enlist enough troops of the right calibre to endure all the hardships. He would have to make it worth their while, at all levels.

William, meanwhile, decided to strengthen his case by an appeal to the courts of Europe for approval. He even approached the Pope, Alexander II, who sent a papal blessing, together with a *gonfanon*, or banner, and according to tradition he also gave William a hair of St Peter, set in a ring, which William was to wear at the battle which he would have to fight. Along with these gifts, the Pope also sent authorisation for William to reform the English Church. In other words, the invasion could be regarded as a holy war.

The arrangements and negotiations took up the best part of seven months, and the duke was not ready until early August, and then he was held up by the weather for another six weeks.

Harold's position in England

Harold, meanwhile, seems to have ignored William's protest. Certainly, he decided to forget about an oath he had taken in 1064, when he was sent by the Confessor to Normandy to confirm Edward's promise of the succession to William, made in 1051. Harold had by this undertaken to support William's claim in the event of Edward's death and, further, swore an oath of fealty to William, doing homage and becoming his vassal, and later received knighthood at his hands, a scene depicted in the Bayeux Tapestry.

We do not know what prompted the *coup d'état*, if such it was, and what pressures were

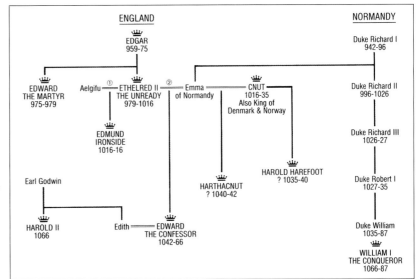

put on Harold to overturn the long-standing promise, but it is known that the Normans were not popular in England, and the leading Anglo-Saxon magnates did not relish the prospect of a Norman King and their own replacement at the top of society by that King's Norman lords. Harold must have felt strong enough to head a movement, as it were to keep England for the English (though England of the mid-eleventh century was hardly the united nation we think of today).

Threats from the North

There were additional complications to come Harold had a half-brother, Tostig, once earl of Northumbria but who had been banished in 1065, who in 1066 organised a series of annoying raids up the English coast, from

ABOVE The ruling families of England and Normandy, showing Duke William's blood relationship with Edward the Confessor and the English throne.

BELOW Duke William makes preparation to invade England. Chain mail is carried to the ships with swords and provisions. A cart laden with weapons and wine is dragged by men preparing to embark.

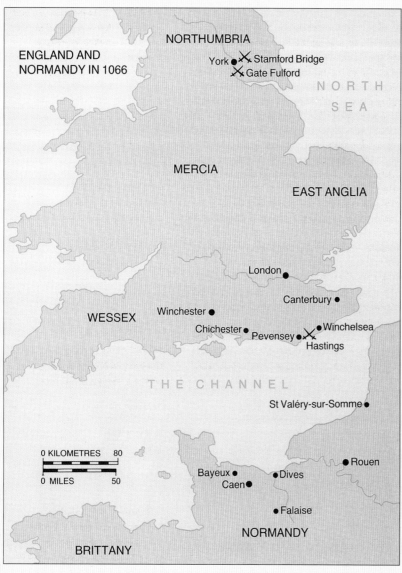

ENGLAND AND
NORMANDY IN 1066

NORTHUMBRIA

York ● ✕ Stamford Bridge
✕ Gate Fulford

NORTH
SEA

MERCIA

EAST ANGLIA

London ●

Canterbury ●

Winchester ●

WESSEX

Chichester ● ● Winchelsea
Pevensey ● ✕
Hastings

THE CHANNEL

St Valéry-sur-Somme ●

0 KILOMETRES   80
0 MILES   50

Rouen ●

Bayeux ●   ● Dives
Caen ●

● Falaise

NORMANDY

BRITTANY

Kent to Northumbria (which at that time comprised most of northern England). Many of these were beaten off by vigorous counter-attack. Tostig then fled to Scotland where sometime during the summer he formed an alliance with the king of Norway, Harold III Hardraada, who had his own claims to the throne of England and who was already planning an invasion of the north.

Harold reacted swiftly to these developments, spurred on by reports of William of Normandy's preparations. Indeed, the danger from Normandy predominated in his dispositions, for he concentrated the main part of his forces in the south, particularly along the coast, and he was taken by surprise when, in mid-September, he heard that Tostig and Hardraada had joined forces in the Humber and were heading up the Ouse towards York.

Harold's preoccupation with defending the south created its own problems. For weeks the contingents of his army and the men of the fleets had to hang about waiting for the Norman invasion. By the beginning of September they had run out of provisions – and probably of patience, too – and the King let them disperse. While they were doing so, the bad news from York reached him.

Tostig and Hardraada reached Gate Fulford, about two miles outside York, and on 20 September took on an army led by Morcar and his brother, Edwin of Mercia, and defeated it. The victors entered York which, as a former Viking capital, still had strong Scandinavian links, and persuaded the arms-bearing citizens to join their force for a march southwards 'to conquer this realm'. This surely suggests that Northumbria was not

solidly behind Harold. Tostig and Hardraada then withdrew from York to the area around Stamford Bridge, about seven miles east.

The battle of Stamford Bridge

Harold reacted swiftly to the first news of the northern invasion, and headed for York, marching by day and night, picking up levies on the way. On 23 or 24 September, he reached Tadcaster, rested and then moved towards York, expecting to engage the invaders, but actually finding that he could march into the city where he learned that his adversaries had gone to Stamford Bridge.

The King continued out on the east side and fell upon his half-brother and Hardraada who were not expecting him. A stubborn struggle ensued, in which both sides fought on foot 'hand to hand and axe to axe', but by the end of the day the Norwegians had been routed and both Tostig and Hardraada slain. It was a tremendous victory, and had there been no danger in the south, it would surely have done much to edge Northumbria closer to the rest of England.

The Normans invade

Two days after Stamford Bridge, on the evening of 27th, William of Normandy at last received the answer to his prayers for favourable winds, and instructed his naval captains to set sail out of the mouth of the Somme and head for the English coast around Pevensey and Hastings.

Duke William had needed the whole seven months to build up his invasion force. To begin with, he had to build a huge fleet of transports, probably as many as 600, to accommodate some 7,000 men including 2–3,000 knights and squires with their horses, as well as arms and supplies. For his own transport, he was presented with a fine flagship, the *Mora*, by his wife Matilda. This is splendidly depicted on the Bayeux Tapestry.

The armada began to assemble in the estuary of the Dives early in August, but after an exasperating month waiting for favourable winds to take it to the English coast, William moved the fleet along the north French coast to St Valéry-sur-Somme, which was outside his domain of Normandy and much closer to England. There, two further frustrating weeks had to pass before the winds were right. He would have had to work hard to keep up the morale of his men, who were by no means all his Norman folk, many coming as volunteers from Picardy, Brittany, Île de France, Flanders and even Aquitaine. Yet this was well within his capability, for among William's great qualities, superb skill in managing men must rank very high. And we cannot overlook the tremendous rewards that lay before his supporters if the adventure succeeded – a whole kingdom of unknown but reputedly immense wealth.

ABOVE Duke William embarks and sets sail with his men and horses in a great armada of ships to England.

OPPOSITE England and Normandy. The battle of Stamford Bridge is shown at the top of the map.

LEFT After their landing at Pevensey the Normans quickly built a bailey castle there, followed by a motte-and-bailey at Hastings.

Then, suddenly but inevitably, the wind did change, on 27 September, and at eventide William ordered the armada to raise anchor and head for England. The next morning the ships beached at Pevensey, unopposed, and almost the first of the duke's acts was to order the construction of a castle within the ruins of one of the old Roman forts of the Saxon Shore, named Anderida by the Romans.

The next day or the day after, William, after leaving a garrison in the castle, moved his forces along to Hastings, a better base, where he raised a second castle not far from the shore, this one a motte-and-bailey castle. You can see a picture of it being built on the Bayeux Tapestry. Meanwhile, all the equipment and supplies for the army were brought ashore as quickly as possible, for it was William's aim to bring the English to battle as soon as he could on ground of his choosing, which meant that Harold – or perhaps Hardraada – must come south to him.

William reached Hastings not knowing how Harold had fared against Hardraada. But he was ready to deal with either as victor. When he did hear of Harold's win at Stamford Bridge, it is reported that he and the English King communicated with each other.

Harold, on his part, heard on 1 or 2 October of William's landing, while he was celebrating Stamford Bridge in York. His response was to ride at once, with such of his army as he could persuade to get on their horses, the whole way to London, nearly 200 miles, covering the distance in about a week. His compatriots were exhausted by the time they reached the capital, but the King did not stop to rest any longer than he needed to call up fresh levies from the Home Counties. Then straightaway he force-marched the makeshift army for 55 or so miles towards Hastings, as keen to engage William as the duke was to challenge him.

Sometime on Friday 13 October, Harold reached what is now Battle, then no more than a ridge marked by a hoary apple-tree, as the Anglo-Saxon Chronicle put it. With him was only part of his army. They camped along and around the ridge overlooking the valley to the south and, it is said, the men spent much of the night drinking and singing – thus adding to their mounting tiredness. Harold hoped that the rest of his forces would arrive the next day.

The final confrontation

News of Harold's arrival at Battle was conveyed to William, still at Hastings, and with it we may be sure a good summary of the English position and the unreadiness of Harold's men. It was a God-given opportunity for the duke to catch his adversary by surprise, and he took it.

At dawn on the Saturday he left his base, heading towards Harold's lines, under cover of darkness. As the sun rose on the Saturday morning, forward scouts of the Norman army could see the English on their ridge, about two miles away. William pressed ahead and by about 8 am had reached Hedgeland on Telham Hill, on the south-east side of Battle. In front of him the ground sloped sharply down to the southern side of the marshy valley below Harold's ridge.

Within an hour the great contest that was to determine the fate of England had begun.

BELOW The Bayeux Tapestry records the unloading of horses from the ships and the departure of soldiers to explore the surrounding countryside

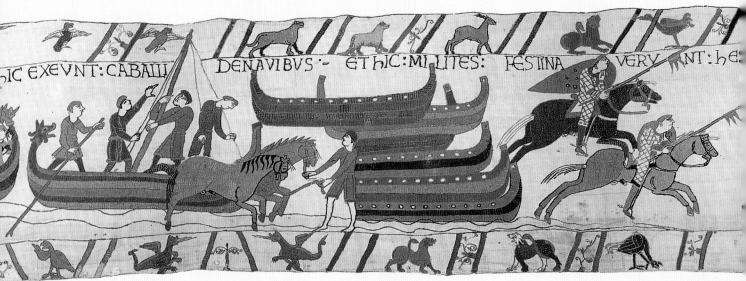

ENGLISH HERITAGE

History of Battle Abbey and its foundation

Atonement for the slaughter of conquest

Battle Abbey was founded in about 1070

In that year the Normans were ordered to do penance for the slaughter incurred in the conquest of England, especially at the battle of Hastings four years earlier. In this spirit William the Conqueror vowed that he would build an abbey where the battle had been fought, and that its high altar would be placed on the spot where King Harold fell.

For centuries it was believed that William had vowed before the great battle that if victorious he would build a monastery on the battlefield (wherever that might be). Now we know that the order to build was not given until 1070, and that even the vow to commemorate the victory with a monastery on the spot where Harold fell can be dated no earlier.

ENGLISH HERITAGE

TOP Illustration by Ivan Lapper showing the consecration of the abbey church by the archbishop of Canterbury in the presence of William Rufus.

ABOVE The seal of Battle Abbey.

In 1070, then, a team of monks was invited to come over from the Benedictine abbey of Marmoutier on the Loire in France to found the abbey. They looked at the site (sloping ground dipping into marshland), expressed their horror at its unsuitability (there was not even any natural water supply on the ridge), and they started to construct buildings further away to the west.

The Conqueror was furious at having his wishes disregarded and ordered the team to go back to the ridge, level it off where needed and build the monastery there. He was not ungenerous to them. He sent ships to Normandy to collect loads of the famous high quality grey-white stone from Caen; he arranged for all the construction bills to be paid by his treasury, and he endowed the new abbey with rich manors and with a

BRITISH LIBRARY

ABOVE Later manuscript portrait of William I, one of four drawings of the Norman Kings of England, each holding a model of a church he founded

BELOW A penny coin of William I.

BRITISH MUSEUM

prosperous church at Cullompton in Devon.

Best of all, he granted the abbot supreme jurisdiction over all the land and people in an area 1½ miles from the abbey church at any one point. This type of grant was called a 'leuga' or league (1½ miles). The privilege meant that the abbey was beyond the control of the bishop in whose see it lay (Chichester, in this case), and the exemption remained unchallenged until the reign of King Stephen (1135–54).

Some time in 1070 or 1071 building work began while the monks occupied temporary wooden buildings nearby. The first structure to rise was the abbey church, the east end of which was finished within six years. The rest of the church was completed by about 1094, when it was consecrated by the archbishop of Canterbury in the presence of the Conqueror's son, William II (Rufus). By the end of the eleventh century various other parts of the monastery had also been finished.

The first abbots consolidate the abbey buildings

We know the names of five abbots who governed the abbey during its first century. Abbot Gausbert (*c*1076–95) built the monks' buildings which may have included a dormitory block in the same place where the remains of the mid-thirteenth-century dorter block still stand (see page 8), and he also built most of the first abbey church. He will have enjoyed the honour of entertaining William II when the church was consecrated.

The next name is Abbot Henry (1096–1102). Then there is a gap, and in 1107 Abbot Ralph from Caen took over until his death in 1124. He completed the first precinct wall (see page 14), and he also put up the stone gate tower, parts of which were much later incorporated into the Great Gatehouse (see page 14). He was succeeded by Abbot Warner (1125–38), in whose time the exemption of Battle Abbey from the jurisdiction of Chichester was first challenged.

Warner was followed by Abbot Walter de Luci (1139–71), whose long abbacy saw the rebuilding of the cloister (see page 10) and its walkways from simple lean-to buildings to a grander square of arcades with marble columns. Abbot Walter was also challenged over the exemption from the Chichester see's jurisdiction, in 1147, by Bishop Hilary of Chichester, who was a skilled lawyer as well as prelate. Walter refused to surrender the rights, whereupon the bishop excommunicated him. Walter appealed to the King, Stephen, while the bishop appealed to the Pope. This escalated a purely local quarrel into a national dispute between the King and the Church, and eventually, in about 1157, the new King of England, Henry II, decided in favour of the abbot.

But there were to be more difficulties. In 1211, Henry II's youngest son, King John (1199–1216), in return for a large cash sum, confirmed the abbey's ancient rights and allowed the monks in future to elect their own abbot This effectively spelled the end of royal

RIGHT Drawing probably made in the early eighteenth century of the Abbey as it may have appeared in about 1737. Sir Anthony Browne's mansion is in the centre, between the gatehouse and guest range. This print, which was published by Ticehurst of Battle, has later pencil annotations.

BRITISH LIBRARY

protection for Battle Abbey's independence.

In 1222 a new bishop was appointed to Chichester, Ralph Nevill, who happened also to be Lord Chancellor. In 1233, Ralph took up the claim to jurisdiction over Battle Abbey and sent in an appeal to the Pope. In 1235 a compromise was reached which, though giving some powers to the bishop, left Battle with most of its independence, and a harmonious relationship appears to have lasted for many years. It was during the thirteenth century, following the compromise, that the abbey was virtually transformed. Most of the buildings were rebuilt, or enlarged, or new ranges added (see section in Tour of the Abbey Ruins, page 8). The main reconstructions appear to have been carried out in two periods, the mid-thirteenth century and the later thirteenth century, but it is not entirely clear in what order the works were done.

New difficulties

The fourteenth century brought problems of a different kind to the abbey community. It was the century in which the Hundred Years War (1337–1453) with France began. While we on this side of the English Channel are inclined, not unnaturally, to recall with pride the great victories of Crécy, Poitiers and elsewhere, and perhaps to think that the fighting was confined to France, it has to be remembered that the French in their turn kept up an almost continuous programme of raids along the south coast of England, seriously disrupting trade and interfering with military installations and harbours.

Defence against these attacks was often left to local land-owners or the Church, and Battle Abbey played an important rôle in organising defence in the Pevensey-Romney area. The most striking evidence of Church involvement in defence in this area is the Great Gatehouse, which was built in 1338–39 (see page 14). The abbey survived the French raids, and indeed in 1377, Abbot Hamo actually led a force of local troops against one raiding party at Winchelsea and saw it off.

The abbey suffered a grievous reduction in its community during the scourge of the Black Death in the middle of the fourteenth century, and it is clear that the numbers of the community never rose again to their original level. Yet there was some rebuilding in the fifteenth century, and the abbey continued to be self-supporting in food as well as continuing to provide help for the poor outside.

BRITISH LIBRARY

The abbey at the Dissolution and afterwards

The end of Battle Abbey as a monastery was inevitable when Henry VIII (1509–47) seriously began to consider dissolving the monasteries of England. The last abbot, John Hamond (1529–38) was described in 1535 by Thomas Cromwell's agent, Richard Layton (sent to inspect monastic establishments prior to their dissolution), as 'the veriest hayne, beetle and buserde and the arentest chorle that ever I see' (the meanest wretch, blockhead and dullard, and the most out-and-out bumpkin I ever met). Layton was no less abusive about the abbey: 'so beggary a house I never see. nor so filthy stuff.' Yet its income in

ABOVE Abbot's great hall, drawn by W H Brooke. The hall is open to visitors only during the school's summer holidays.

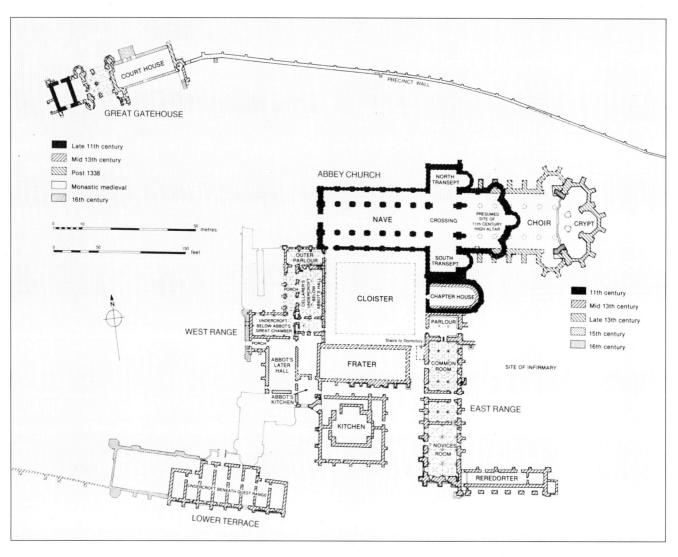

GREAT GATEHOUSE

COURT HOUSE

PRECINCT WALL

Late 11th century
Mid 13th century
Post 1338
Monastic medieval
16th century

0   10   50 metres
0   50   150 feet

N

ABBEY CHURCH

NORTH TRANSEPT

NAVE   CROSSING   PRESUMED SITE OF 11th CENTURY HIGH ALTAR   CHOIR   CRYPT

SOUTH TRANSEPT

OUTER PARLOUR

PORCH   CELLARER'S UNDERCROFT BELOW   ABBOT'S HALL

UNDERCROFT BELOW ABBOT'S GREAT CHAMBER

PORCH

CLOISTER

CHAPTER HOUSE

PARLOUR

Stairs to Dormitory

WEST RANGE

ABBOT'S LATER HALL

ABBOT'S KITCHEN

FRATER

COMMON ROOM

SITE OF INFIRMARY

EAST RANGE

KITCHEN

NOVICES ROOM

REREDORTER

11th century
Mid 13th century
Late 13th century
15th century
16th century

UNDERCROFT BENEATH GUEST RANGE

LOWER TERRACE

Detailed ground plan of the abbey church and buildings, showing the building phases

1535 was £880 a year, one of the highest of the Benedictine establishments. When dissolution did come in 1538, Abbot Hamond was pensioned off with £100 a year.

In the same year the abbey and much of the land was given by the King to Sir Anthony Browne who razed the church to the ground and pulled down the chapter house and part of the cloisters, and made the outer courtyard the main courtyard. The west range which included the abbot's house was converted into a mansion for himself.

Browne also rebuilt the guest range over the undercrofts of the medieval guest range, and gave the new range two decorated stair turrets. This building was almost 200 ft long. It is supposed to have been intended as a residence for Henry VIII's son and heir, Prince Edward (later, Edward VI) and his half-sister Princess Elizabeth (later, Elizabeth I), but neither of the royal children ever lived there.

The estate remained with the Browne family until 1715 when it was sold to Sir Thomas Webster, in whose family it stayed (with an interval between 1857 and 1901) until 1976 when it was saved for the nation with a generous donation from the United States of America. The battlefield and abbey ruins are now looked after by English Heritage.

During the Webster ownership, the abbey's fortunes varied. In the mid-eighteenth century the Tudor guest range was demolished and only the two turrets survived. At the end of the eighteenth century the mansion part was improved, and it was added to in the nineteenth century.

After the First World War (1914–18), the mansion was leased to Battle Abbey School, which still occupies it. In 1931 the building was gutted in a fire, but its important rooms were carefully restored under the direction of the architect Sir Harold Brakespear.